7 SECRETS TO GET YOUR DREAM LIFE

7 SECRETS TO GET YOUR DREAM LIFE

written by

NILESH GOSWAMI

ADHYYAN BOOKS

7 Secrets to Get Your Dream Life

1st Edition

Publication Date: August 2018
Price: ₹350 | $14.99
ISBN: 978-93-87502-72-7

Published by:
Adhyyan Books
Office No. 637,
Opposite Vivanta by Taj,
DDA SFS. Pocket-1, Dwarka,
Sec-22, New Delhi-110077
Website: http://adhyyanbooks.com
E-mail: contact@adhyyanbooks.com

Dedication

Dedicated to my Guru Swami Hans ji, my mentor Mr. Ram Verma, my parents- Mrs. Shakuntla Goswami and Mr. Harpal Goswami, my wonderful wife Shivani, & my lovely sons- Supash and Shiven

Acknowledgments

God has blessed me with a lot of wonderful and lovely people in my life without whom, I could not have written my dream book. I would like to express my gratitude to all of them for their support and love.

First, I am indebted to my Guru Swami Hans ji who has shown me the path to live the life. His unconditional love and support is matchless. I am thankful to my mentor Mr. Ram Verma who has been guiding me with his valuable advice from time to time. It is because of his guidance that I could become a successful life coach.

There is no word to express my gratitude towards my parents Smt. Shakuntla Goswami and Sh. Harpal Goswami. Whatever they have done for me, I could never repay. They ensure to provide me with a conducive atmosphere at home and always encourage me in moving ahead in the life.

I would like to thank my wife Shivani for her patience, and moral support. She has always stood behind me in all of my endeavours. It would not be incorrect to say she is the backbone of the family. I would also like to thank my adorable sons Supash and Shiven for all their love.

I am also thankful to all other family members and friends who have always been a source of inspiration for me.

I would also like to thank Mr. Nitin Soni, CEO of Adhyyan Books and his team- especially Mr. Vikas Gaur to make this book a great success.

Foreword

When Nilesh invited me to write the foreword for his book "7 Secrets to Get Your Dream Life", it was a matter of pride and pleasure for me as his mentor. I know him for a long time as a highly committed, knowledgeable, and enthusiastic person who completes his job with a passion which you will see in this book as well.

As an NLP Wellness Life Coach, I can state that this book is going to leave a notable impact on the lives of the people. Each one of us is entitled to get a life one wants. But we face so many challenges related to our health, relationships, finances, career, etc. These challenges can be because of issues related to the past, present or uncertainty of the future. We live with many limiting beliefs, and patterns of negativity which prevent us from achieving the higher levels in the life. However, we can overcome these challenges. The key lies in our mind. Our mind has unlimited power. Either we are ignorant, or we do not know how to use this power. What we will be, depends upon how well we use our mind. If we learn to reprogram the subconscious mind and align the conscious and subconscious mind, we can get the desired results.

This is a wonderful book which will help you in understanding the mind and tapping its unlimited potential. The techniques mentioned in the book are so simplified that everyone can understand and learn them with no pre-required knowledge. Once you learn these techniques, you will be the master of your subconscious mind and will open the vast treasures hidden inside you. This book will not only empower your life to overcome the challenges but also help you find the purpose of your life.

Ram Verma

NLP Wellness Life Coach

Preface

Looking at the Himalayas, from the verandah of my home near Kasauli (a small hill station in the Himalayas), I was admiring the beauty and peace of the mighty Himalayas. Never ever in my life, I had been at so much peace I was in the last few years. It's a dream come true that I have been leading a life which I had always aspired. It was only a few years back when I had lost the track of my dreams; in fact, had lost confidence in myself but with Guru's grace, came back on track. Universe helped me in a way I got access to certain techniques which is still unknown to a common person. When I implemented these techniques, these set everything right in place for me.

As a life coach, I conduct workshops and counsel people which means I need to interact with people and groups. But I had a limiting belief that " Public speaking is not my cup of tea." Over the years I had developed a fear of going on the stage. This was the major roadblock to live my dream life. To add to my worries, I had an insecurity complex which had made me short-tempered. But you don't know these things until you introspect yourself. Fortunately, I had a turning point in my life which made me conduct a complete internal audit. Moreover, I found my Guru who helped me to come out of my issues. In this process, I came to know how our mind functions and how can we use it for achieving almost anything. If we can establish congruence between the conscious and subconscious mind, we can do wonders which normally we cannot even visualize. Using these powerful methods, not only could I overcome my stage fear, insecurity, and my temperament but also cured my obesity, high blood pressure, cholesterol, and sugar levels. Even my eyesight got improved. Though I had only targeted for my weight reduction, everything else came as a complimentary gift.

During this time, I realized the enormous potential of the mind. Post this, I completed my certifications for stress management, NLP (Neuro-Linguistic Programming), and Memory Trainer. It was during this time I met my Mentor Mr. Ram Verma who is India's leading NLP Wellness Life Coach. He helped me in honing my skills and I could reach the level where I am today. Today, I have been helping many people to come out of their life issues and lead a wonderful life. Apart from one-on-one coaching, I am conducting workshops so that more people get to know this wonderful technique. My mission is to make these techniques available to each household so that everyone can get benefitted. When I know something, what is the use of limiting it to myself only? Universe has given this to me and now it is my turn to give back to others. This mission inspired me to write this book so that everyone is not only aware of the immense power of mind but also get to know how to use it to achieve even impossible looking targets. In this book, I am unearthing seven secrets which you must know to fulfill your dreams and desires. This book is for everyone whether you are an entrepreneur, working professional, sportsperson, actor, singer, student or even homemaker. Once you apply these secrets on yourself, you will realize the enormous power of the mind.

This book is not just a book, but a live workshop where you can learn those secrets which you have been longing for a long time. These secrets have helped me a lot to live a life of my choice and I am sure these will help you too. I am confident that if you follow these secrets religiously without analyzing too much, you'll be able to achieve your dreams. Once you master these secrets, there will not be any looking back and you will be the master of your mind which will help you in shaping your life as you want. I would suggest you go through the book thoroughly to get the maximum benefit.

Nilesh Goswami
Stress Management Professional,
NLP Coach and Memory Trainer

Contents

C. Create Your Zone of Excellence

Part 3: Time to Act

PART 1

Understanding the Mind

CHAPTER 1

Why do We Suffer?

Have you ever heard "Desires are the cause of sufferings"? In fact, these are not the desires but failure to fulfill desires or expectations that cause one to suffer. We cannot fulfill our desires because of two reasons. One is you perceive that you cannot do so, and the other is when you are so occupied in doing other things you forget what you really want to achieve.

Human beings are not born to suffer; we are born to experience the joy and ecstasy in life. But the problem is that most of the people do not know how to fulfill their dreams. The result is that they start discounting their dreams to lessen the sufferings only to make them suffer even more.

Each one of us would like to achieve the best. If I ask you a question what do you want in life? Those who do not have the money or strive for more, will say they need money. Those who are suffering from some health issues will strive for good health. People having relationship issues would need better relationships. And those who are under stress would look for peace of mind. Some need only one of these; some may need more while others may need all. Everyone wants to move to the next higher level be it money, health, relationship or peace of mind.

But how many can really reach that level- only a few. What is the difference between them and others? Why some people remain ordinary while others reach extraordinary levels. Do they have better skills or is their environment better than the others or are their behaviours better? Maybe many of people who remain ordinary have better skills, capabilities, environment, or behaviours. Still, they do not excel and reach those levels what they are capable of. So, what is the difference between these people and other people who are cursing their environment or destiny for the outcomes they get in their life?

Who stops us from realizing our dreams?

It is none other than our mind itself. In fact, the root cause is the way we use our mind. When we do not control our mind, it controls us. Mind is just a tool provided to us for our support. It is a bio-computer which functions as per the software installed in it. When there is a bug in the software, it affects the output. When we input garbage, then what else can we expect other than garbage. These are the two ways when the output is not the desired one. This garbage is all sort of negativities and unwanted things which we keep on putting in our mind. Bugs can be due to limiting beliefs, our experiences, past events, environment, past results etc. The way we perceive events makes all the difference.

However, the good news is that we can reprogram this software, clear all the bugs and run the program of life swiftly. By correct programming of our mind, we can achieve many such things which we'd have thought difficult to achieve. We see many live examples where people even with a physical disability have reached the top position in their field. So, differentiator here is the way we use our mind. To understand it better, let us understand what the mind is.

CHAPTER 2

Mind - the Differentiator

In this physical world, God has given a beautiful machine to us to operate which if we use intelligently can make us do wonders. But if we use it casually, it may overpower us. Now you have guessed it right. This machine is nothing but our mind. How do we use our mind decides what we will be? It's also said in Buddhist quotes that

"The mind is everything.
What you think you become."

—Buddha

So, what matters is how do you use your mind. Before knowing the secret - how to use our mind to get the dream life, let us first understand how does it actually function?

The mind operates with its five helpers which we call our five senses - visual sense, auditory sense, kinesthetic sense (feeling), gustatory (taste) and olfactory (smell). There are three levels of the human mind- Conscious, subconscious and unconscious. Here do not confuse unconscious with the medical term 'unconscious' which has a different meaning.

The conscious mind operates using the five senses. At this moment you are seeing this book that means you are using the visual sense of your conscious mind. In the same way, if you are listening to music, you are doing it with the auditory sense of your conscious mind; and if you are touching this book to see if it is smooth or rough that is your kinesthetic sense at work. you use your gustatory sense while eating food and olfactory while smelling something. While perceiving an event we generally use three senses- visual, auditory and kinesthetic. We do not use the other two senses (gustatory and olfactory) while perceiving an event except for some specific events.

The Subconscious mind also has five senses. At this moment you can see your house or office or another thing/place in your imagination. Well, that's the visual sense of the subconscious mind. You can hear the voice of your boss or your wife in your mind; have the feelings of past incidents- both pleasant and unpleasant - within your body; have tastes and smell of many things stored in your mind. These are due to these five senses of the Subconscious mind.

Let's understand this in a better way. Imagine that you are entering your house. You are opening the door of your house. Now you get inside and go the kitchen. Open the door of your refrigerator and pick a lemon. Now, take a knife and cut the lemon. Squeeze the juice of lemon inside your mouth. Don't tell me that you are feeling the taste of the lemon. You have not even touched the lemon, then from where this sour taste is coming. This is because it was stored in your mind already. You could see your house with clarity as it was also stored somewhere in your mind. This information gets stored in your subconscious mind.

The subconscious mind is 50% to 60% of your mind and unconscious mind is 30% to 40% of mind. Thus, subconscious and unconscious mind represents 90% of the total mind. That is why we call that the conscious mind is just the tip of the iceberg while the main iceberg (subconscious + unconscious) is inside the water. The subconscious mind is much more powerful than the conscious mind.

Both subconscious and unconscious mind are the storehouses of information given by the conscious mind. The only difference between the two is that the subconscious mind stores all the recent information while unconscious has all deep routed information since our birth. Now onwards wherever I'll be using the term subconscious, it will be for both subconscious and unconscious.

Let's think mind as a computer. In fact, it is a bio-computer only and is much more powerful than any computer existing in this universe. We can consider the conscious mind as the screen of the computer and the subconscious mind as RAM (Random Access Memory) of the computer where data is stored. Thus, the subconscious mind is a storehouse of all the memories, beliefs, attitudes, behaviours etc. It has taken all these things from the conscious mind and stored in it.

In another analogy, we can consider the subconscious mind as a horse and the conscious mind as its rider. Now wherever rider says, it'll go. That means whatever it has taken from the conscious mind and stored in its storehouse, it'll act accordingly. If you have stored all the negativity, limiting beliefs etc., it'll act as per that. If there is no congruence between the conscious and subconscious mind, then it'll be like the horse is going as per its own wish as the rider is not controlling it.

Whatever your conscious mind feels it should remember, it hands over that data to the subconscious mind for permanent storage. As a loyal storekeeper, the subconscious mind keeps all the information along with the emotions which the conscious mind has attached to it. So, you need to be careful what you are giving to the subconscious mind. If you pick a pen and call it as an atom bomb, the subconscious mind will store this information as something dangerous and will keep on alerting the conscious mind in form of fear, stress, worry, diseases, etc.

But if the conscious mind has positive feelings attached to an information, it gets reflected in confidence, happiness etc. Apart from this subconscious mind takes care of all the physiological functions such as breathing, heartbeat etc. for which we need not focus. Now we know about the mind, we will next find out how do we perceive events and how this perception is the real cause of what we are.

CHAPTER 3

How does Perception Lead to the Destiny?

As we have discussed in the previous chapters that the subconscious mind is a storehouse and keeps on communicating with the conscious mind to fill its warehouse. That means whatever we are putting into the subconscious mind, it will program us accordingly. Now the process is not that simple. Because the language of the subconscious mind differs from that of the conscious mind. The conscious mind communicates through speech, words, writing, thoughts, etc. while the subconscious mind communicates via emotions, feelings, sensations, reflexes, images, and dreams. Our mind sees the external information through a lens. It then applies a filter before storing the information in the subconscious mind.

Imagine you are planning to visit the Eiffel Tower along with your friends. One of your friends cannot go with the group as he is not well. So, he stays back. You all enjoy a lot there and come back to your hotel. When you come back, the friend who could not go for site seeing is curious to know about the Eiffel Tower. So, he asks each one of you about it. What do you think- Will all of you be describing it in the same way? After all, it is about the same event. But to his surprise, each one of you is narrating differently – in your own way. Even though the Eiffel Tower is unique, but its experience is different for different persons. That means everyone has different software running in their mind which is processing the information in its own way.

You can put it in another way. We all see the world through an imaginary lens and the information which passes through this lens get filtered out by deletion, distortion, and generalization. Our mind does this based on our past patterns, beliefs, values, our environment, etc.

Deletion is the process by which mind deletes a lot of information. When you go from your home to office, you see a lot of things – trees, people, vehicles, buildings, etc. In a panoramic view, our mind captures over two million information. But how many of these do we remember? Hardly any or maybe five to seven when we consciously try to remember or if we see some unique thing. Here mind deletes all the other information as it considers them to be irrelevant.

Distortion is nothing but changing the meaning of something. Here we are not discussing good or bad. It's only that we change the meaning of an information or event. For example, if someone says, "Today temperature is 45 degree Celsius." Let us assume that it is a fact for that day. Then he says that the weather is bad today. Here, he has changed the meaning of the information from 45 degree Celsius to bad weather. This is the distortion.

Generalization is making a general statement or concept which we inference from specific cases. Let us assume a class of fifty students in which five students are making a lot of noise. Just because of these five students you are labelling the class as a bad class. We generalize so many things as per our internal software which many times is too far from the reality and that becomes the reason for our pains and sufferings.

When you and your friends visited the Eiffel Tower, all of you have gone through this process of deletion, distortion, and generalization. This made the subjective experience of the event (Eiffel) different for all of you. This subjective experience is a person's own reality which may not be the same as that of the actual event. In fact, most of the time it differs from the objective event. Therefore, the reality of everyone is different. That's why we say- "No one is Wrong. They only have a different way of thinking".

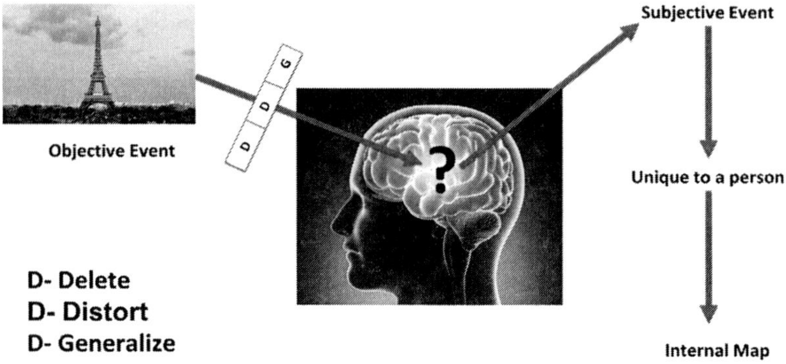

Though the event is the same, the reality of that event in our mind that is, the subjective experience of the actual event is unique for every person. This subjective experience is based on our experiences, beliefs etc. stored in our subconscious mind. And this subjective experience is in form of images, movies, sounds, feelings etc. Depending upon the intensity of subjective experiences, these pictures will have bright or dull colours (visual sense), sounds (auditory sense) may be loud or low, feelings (kinesthetic sense) may get intensified or low and so on. If we perceive an event as a bad event which is stored in bright colourful movies with loud sounds and intensified feelings, chances are that we get affected heavily because of that event. But, if it is the other way around, that is if the movie is dull or black and white, sounds are low and feelings are also low, then these events might not be hurting us that much.

One thing is clear now that the root cause of sufferings lies in the internal map (the subjective experience) we have created. This internal map creates the state of mind. This state is nothing but known as our mood more commonly. For players, you call it 'form' while for musicians it is better known as 'groove'. This state of mind can be resourceful or unresourceful. Resourceful state of mind refers to love, happiness, ecstasy, confidence, cheerfulness, flexibility, wellness etc. while sadness, frustration, anger, anxiety, stress, illness etc. are the examples of the unresourceful state of mind.

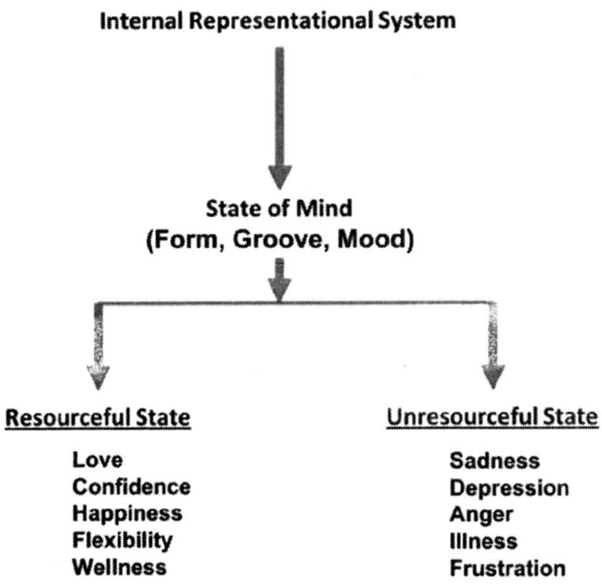

When we are in our resourceful state we have access to all of our resources while we cannot access even our own resources in the unresourceful state. Resourceful state signifies that we have resolved our issues while unresourceful state points out that some issues are still unresolved and we need to address them immediately. That is why we stay in a stuck state or fight-or-flight mode when we have issues to resolve. In this state, we cannot use our creativity as the mind is engaged in firefighting all the time. Apart from this, during fight-or-flight mode stress hormones gets released which if not compensated by the body give rise to psychosomatic diseases.

Whatever state we are in, it gets reflected in our behaviour and actions. We do wonders if we are in a good state and invite disaster in a bad state of mind. Hence, our karmas (i.e. behaviours or actions) decides what results do we get, and that shapes our destiny.

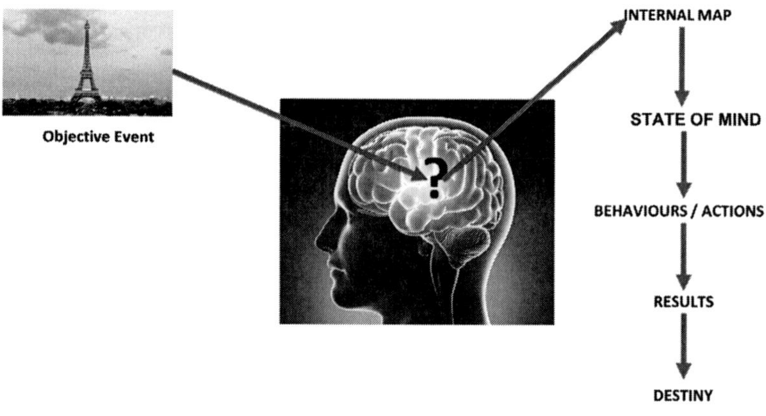

These outcomes can pertain to any sphere of life - health, career, finances, relationships, etc. If we need to get a positive outcome that is if we want our health at the best, flying career, heavy bank balances, and good relationships, we need to learn to be in a good state of mind.

Can we do this at will? Yes, we can. For that we need to see what is it that creates the resourceful state - it is the internal map of the events stored in our subconscious mind. So, if we can reprogram our subconscious mind as we do with our computer's software, we can change the internal map and hence the state. Can we change the state at once? Oh yes! See the example of a cricket game. A batsman has not been making runs in his few past innings and he gets labelled as out of form. But suddenly in a match, he hits a century, and the form is back. Similarly, the spirit of a cricket team may be low when opponent team is making lots of runs and the team is not succeeding in taking wickets. But the moment they get a wicket, you can see the change in their behaviours. Now the chance of taking another wicket increases many folds. What is all that? They have just changed their state which changed their behaviour. Obviously, the results will also be better.

In fact, when you learn to keep your state of mind always up, you can even find opportunities out of the crisis.

"The Fastest way to grow in life is to
find out opportunities from the crisis."

—Nilesh Goswami

In the subsequent chapters, you will learn the secret but simple techniques to reprogram your subconscious mind. Using these techniques, you will replace the patterns of negativity and limiting beliefs into patterns of positivity, opportunities and success. You will be then moving toward the destiny which you have seen in your dreams. At that point of time, no power of this universe can be a roadblock to your dream life. In fact, all the energy of the universe will support you in achieving your mission - the mission to get your dream life. So, fasten your belt to unearth the 7 secrets which will ultimately take you to your dream life. I have divided these seven secrets into three categories:

1. *Create Blueprints of Dream life:* The very first thing is to know what we want from this life. Once you do this, you may see objections which hinder your progress. So, the next step is to clear all the objections.

2. *Create a Strong Foundation:* Once you are clear of your destination, it is time to strengthen your foundation by making yourself resilient.

3. *Create your Zone of Excellence:* Here you will learn the techniques which will help you in excel in all sphere of life so that you have a smooth journey to reach your dream destination.

PART 2

7 Secrets

A

Create Blueprints of Your Dream Life

CHAPTER 4

Secret #1: Know Your Dreams and Create the Masterplan

Know Your Dreams

It was cold freezing morning during winters when as usual I reached airport well before time. I was travelling from Delhi to Mumbai to conduct a workshop. After the security check, I went to the lounge to have my breakfast. I checked my watch; it was still time. So, I started roaming around and after some time reached the gates. Gates were yet not open, so I sat on a chair in the waiting area. Everyone was waiting peacefully for the announcement of the gate opening. Some were reading books, some were chatting while some others were constantly looking at the gates. Then I saw a guy who stood up and went towards the gates. Not to my surprise, other people also started walking behind him and soon there was a long queue. By the way, the announcement for opening the gates was not yet made.

I am sure all of you must have observed these kinds of situations at different places. Why does this happen? People were sitting peacefully until this guy stood up and all of them started following him. You all know what it is called– The Herd Mentality. Don't you think we all are a victim of this mentality at least to some extent? We do things which others are doing, without even thinking whether it is leading to our desired path. After some time, we get bored and frustrated.

I have many friends who come to me and say "hey buddy! Don't know why am I doing this job?" This happens when people go in a direction opposite to where they actually wanted to go. Moreover, they don't even know they are going in the wrong direction. Their dreams are buried deep somewhere in their subconscious and they are busy doing things which everyone else is doing. This is the story of most of us. We don't listen to ourselves. We are just not ourselves.

There are so many people whom we think they have reached a level and achieved so many things, yet they are not happy. Maybe it is not their destination; they have just reached there while walking on the path of life as everyone else in the crowd has been doing. Their real destination may be somewhere else. Everyone is running his own race and hence has a different destination. Still, we all seem to run in one direction. Amazing! Isn't it? Do you all know you are in the right direction or not? Suppose you are in the right direction, how would you know you have reached the destination. For that, one must first know one's destination. This destination is nothing but our dream life. But how many of us know consciously what their dream life is? Our dream life is our deep and intense desires which we want to achieve in our life. But being overwhelmed by the life, many of us forget at the conscious level what their desires were, and these intense desires take a back seat somewhere deep into our subconscious mind to give way to other so-called important issues.

Where will such a life lead us to? You know it better. That is why we get frustrated and unhappy even after achieving so many things. The first thing we should do is to know our dreams. Once we know our dreams, we get to know whether we are in the right direction. Then we can plan on how to get our dream life.

You need to explore what you desire in this life. What is the purpose of your life? Many people say they want to do it, but they do not have time. My goodness! you don't have time to know what you want from this life. You will keep thinking I'll live my life once certain commitments are over. Well, friends, these will never be over. If one thing gets over, another will come, then another and another. And then the day will come when you'll have to depart from this world. That day you'll think, "Hope, I would have lived the way I wanted," and you'll leave with a heavy heart and with lots of desires. Do you want this to happen to you? I am sure you would not.

It's high time now. Just get ready today and explore what you want from life. You need to explore this yourself as you are the best person in this universe who knows what you truly want. What is your dream life? Explore your inner desires. It may be teaching, training people, entertaining people, discovering new possibilities, social work, painting, writing a book, helping people, inventing new things or it may be so many other beautiful things you'd like to do. When I explored myself and came to know what I wanted, I left the prestigious Indian Engineering Services job which is a dream for every engineer in India. I did not want to move in a direction which is taking me in a direction opposite to my dreams. When this happens, it is always advisable to take two actions. One, stop right there as there is no point in moving in a wrong direction. It will do nothing but to create more distance between you and your dream life. Second, explore in what way can you move in the right direction? So, I started working on my dreams and made a systematic plan to get out of where I had stuck. It took me another ten years after this to get out of the mess I was living in.

So, just explore what you want from this life to make it wonderful and beautiful. When you will start exploring your interests, loves, desires, passions, you will start feeling the excitement. Let me help you in this exploration. I give you a simple technique to unearth your deep intense desires. Relax yourself by taking a couple of deep breaths. Close your eyes and scan your body from toes to the head as if you are seeing your body from outside.

Once you are done, take a pen and paper. Sit comfortably at some place where no one distracts you. Now start writing in what way you want to spend your remaining life. Just one caution that "do not use your logical mind to test anything". Imagine that everything you are thinking, is possible and you have all the resources available to you. While writing you'll not stop in between. Continue writing without thinking and in a natural flow. You need to write for minimum 20 minutes. Now you have your first draft ready. You have now ignited your deep desires lying in the subconscious mind. Your subconscious will now start giving you many other things which you have missed out in the draft. When you get them, keep on adding them to your draft and in a few days, you will have a complete picture of what you expect from your life. Once you know your dreams, the next step is to make a foolproof plan.

The Masterplan

Now you know what you want from your life, the next step is to check out the objections you are getting from your internal as well as external environment. You need to question your plan now. Why do you want the life you have just explored? This 'WHY' is the most important thing. You got to know the reason. Stronger the reason, stronger will be your chances to achieve the desired result. At present state, you have some gains and some pains. Likewise, when you get your dream life, you will have pains and gains. Pains here may be the effort you need to do to get your dream life while pain at present state may be because you are in a stuck state and not able to achieve what you desire. You have the gains at the present level as well. Whatever these pains and gains are, identify them. For example, if a person wants to quit smoking, the gains at present state maybe he gets relaxed when he is in tension or he gets the company of his friends. Pains here may be the health issue because of smoking or maybe the family does not like this behaviour. Likewise, gains at the desired state will be good health. Apart from this, he will get more affection and love from his family. He will live longer to take care of his family and enjoy with them. However, there may be certain pains also when he quits smoking. He may perceive that he might lose the company of his friends with whom he chats while smoking.

Whatever these gains and pains are at present level and the desired level i.e. when you get your dream life, identify them. Find out what will be the gains in the short term and long term which you will get once you get your dream life. There should be some emotional connection to what you want to achieve. Without emotional connect you'd not get motivated to achieve the dreams. In the same way, identify what are the pains at present level which you will avoid by achieving this. Your gains, once you achieve your dream life and your pains at present, must be much greater than the gains you are having at present and pains you need to undergo for the change. Only then you will get motivated for your desired goal. Once your 'WHY' is clear and is strong enough, you are good to go.

Once your reason to achieve your desired life is clear, plan properly how to get your dreams. The first step is to ensure that you are moving in the right direction. Create evidences which tell you constantly that you are moving in the right direction. e.g. if you are travelling from Delhi to Chandigarh, you know that Panipat, Karnal, Ambala etc. will come in between. So, if you see that these places are coming, you are going in the right direction. However, if you reach Jaipur, you know it is in the opposite direction. You at once know you are in the wrong direction and need to correct it. Therefore, just ensure that you are moving in the right direction by creating these kinds of evidences.

Next is you should know when you have achieved your dreams. So, decide in advance when you consider that you have achieved the desired goal. To whom will you be with and where will you be when you reach your destination. Do this homework in advance.

Next step is to ask yourself how you would get them. What are the resources you will need? Do you have all those resources? These resources can be internal such as confidence, flexibility, right attitude or these may be external such as money, finances. Check whether you have all these or need to gain. If you do not have, you have to gain these resources. If you don't get them, you cannot fulfill your dreams.

Whenever you are on the path to your dream life, make sure you have the direct control. If you let others control you or think if others help me then only I can move forward, then it will create obstacles for you. It will be like that if someone wants to get slim and says I can only get slim if there is a gym near my place. Here the person depends on others for the fulfillment of desires. He is at the mercy of the others. Hope you are getting what I want to convey. Taking help from someone is a different thing but giving control of your life to others is different. Keep the control with you only. After all, this is your dream life.

When you are on your dream journey, there may be objections. These objections may be internal or external. Before moving forward, you need to clear these objections. An internal objection may be in form of two internal voices which have different views. It may be like there are two parts inside you – one is giving you a clear signal to go ahead, and the other is stopping you. In that case, if you go ahead, then it will be at the cost of second part losing the game. Both of these are your own part only. If anyone of them loses, it is your loss. You need to clear this objection. In such a scenario, just imagine that you take out both the parts in your hand and communicate with both as a mediator. First, you ask the second part who is having the objection that what is it you are not allowing me to go ahead. Then this part will tell you what is the objection. It will communicate with you as it is your part only and at the back of your mind you also know what the objection is. This objection may be a conflict in values or beliefs or there may be pains in leaving the current state. Whatever be the reason, this part will let you know. Then you ask, is there a way I can pursue this dream with no objection? Here you are asking for alternatives. When you are asking the part for alternatives, indirectly you are commanding your subconscious to find out the alternatives and your subconscious knows what is good for you. It will come out with alternatives. Do not expect it to give alternatives immediately. Once you give the command to your subconscious, it will come out with answers in some time. It can be instant, and it can take a few days also, but it will, for sure, come out with alternatives. Be sure to give commands just before you go to sleep so that your subconscious is working on it all the night. Once you get the alternative ways to achieve the dreams, then you go to the first part for its permission for the alternative. If the first part does not agree with any of the alternatives, ask the first part to look for more alternatives. Continue this process till both the parts are in an agreement. Once both parts agree, you merge both and integrate with you again. This way you can handle the internal objection. There may be more than one objection. You need to resolve all the internal objections before moving further.

Likewise, clear all the external objections as well. Check out what impact the path you have chosen for your dream life will have on the people significant to you? How will they feel? Will they get hurt? Clear these objections in the same way as you have done above. Assure them you are on the right path and show them the long-term benefits. They will agree unless there is a conflict in their values and beliefs. If there is such a conflict, check out for alternative paths or even ask them for the alternatives. Once you get the alternatives, go ahead with them. You can also visualize that they are sitting in front of you and a white or golden light is falling on all of you. Imagine that you are clarifying all the details and ensuring them you are on the right path and in the long run, it will be helpful.

Once you do this, the next important step is to identify yourself with dreams. If you are not identifying yourself with your dreams, you will not have enough motivation to achieve them. This means you live your dreams with the day one. You behave as if you have already achieved the dream. For example, if someone wants to get rich, and he is having the middle-class mentality, will he be successful in his goal? I tell you, he will not. Because unless he makes his identity as a rich person in the subconscious mind, the subconscious mind will not accept that as a goal. Therefore, it is very important that you identify yourself as you dream yourself to be, from the day one.

Now, it's time to break down your dreams into milestones as our mind is comfortable with small things. It gets scared seeing large pieces. Imagine you tell a student to memorize a ten-page essay. The student will get scared to see such a long essay. But if you give him one paragraph at a time, he will easily memorize all the paragraphs one by one and thus the complete essay.

Next is to make a mental movie of achieving all the milestones. Run this mental movie every day in your mind preferably in the morning and just before you go to sleep. This will keep your subconscious mind busy in channelizing the energy of this universe to help you realize your dreams. Now with all the planning done and objections cleared, it's time to take actions as per your plan. Unless you act, you will not achieve your dreams. The first thing to do now is to strengthen your foundation which we will learn in the next chapters. Without a strong foundation, one cannot make a strong building. I'll give you the techniques by which you can make it strong, so you can traverse on your journey smoothly.

B

Create a Strong Foundation

CHAPTER 5

Secret #2: Clear the Garbage

Though you have cleared the objections which you had in your plan, still there may be something which can hold you back and prevent from moving ahead on the journey to the wonderful life. These are the past traumatic experiences, events and unpleasant things lie deep down in our mind. In a normal scenario, they are lying dormant and remain inaccessible to the conscious mind. But on a similar trigger which caused that situation, these events are surfaced up. For example, when you listen to an old song, you suddenly start experiencing past emotions associated with it. The song here is the trigger. Likewise, something can trigger an unpleasant event of the past. This is like a file stored in the computer having a password. When you enter the file using the correct password, you can unlock it. Same happens in case of these deeply routed events as well. When a similar situation occurs and acts as a password to an event, the event gets freshened up in your memory. When this happens, you relive that event. The internal map in form of movies, sounds, and feelings, is now LIVE in the mind. You have the same feelings as you were having during that event. If you have just triggered a bad, traumatic event, this can be disastrous. When you feel those pains, you immediately go into an unresourceful state of mind. Well, you know now what that means. You cannot perform what you are capable of. Because now you have the reference to a past event which communicates with your conscious mind and gives the negative signal about it.

For example, if a student is going to an examination and the moment he takes the seat, he gets a signal from the subconscious mind you will not clear the exam because you had failed last time. Same is the case with a person who is going for an interview or going for an important boardroom presentation. The mind has already accepted the defeat even before putting an effort. How can a person succeed in that case? Imagine this in case of handling relationships, finances or even health. Will you be able to excel in these fields? You won't.

Each of us is carrying this past burden in the mind and this burden is marring our present. Though some of you may say, "I do not have any such past burden in my mind", it may not be true. At this moment you cannot recall in the absence of a trigger. But when some situation triggers it similar to the situation responsible for the event in the past, you'll feel the pain. You may think of a recent past when you were feeling pain. That might help you in remembering any such incidence.

If you carefully look at the spelling of Present, it says 'Pre / Sent'. So, if you are sending good things from past, the present will be like a gift else it will lead to all sort of negativity, failures and what not. Now the choice is with you whether you want to keep carrying this burden and the life will move on as it is going on at present. Or else, you can decide to remove this unnecessary burden and not only improve the present but also make the future beautiful.

Let me narrate my story. Since childhood, I had an insecurity complex, and I was unaware of the reason behind it. It used to get reflected in my behaviour as I could trust no one and saw everyone with a suspicious eye. I used to remain in a fear of losing whether it is my job, relationships or money. I thought what could cause this behaviour of mine. I got no answer, and I remained in the fear of losing things. It had shaken my confidence. Every time I had a meeting with my boss or MD, I used to go to the meeting room with fear in my mind. The same thing happened at home. I always had a fear of losing my family. And the major problem I faced due to this fear was that I was never what I was. Moreover, I used to shout a lot when I didn't know what to do. And these things made the situation worse for me. I had even developed a high blood pressure apart from being in anxiety all the time.

After learning these secrets to get the dream life, I decided to use them on myself. When I gave the command to my subconscious mind, I found the reason, though not instantly. The reason was a painful burden I was carrying since the age of five. I stood first in my class and the result was also declared. But when there was the ceremony, they changed the result and placed me at second rank. Son of an influential person in that area was given the first position. That event shattered me from inside. I was, after all, a small kid only. I kept crying for the whole day. My parents tried to make me understand that it does not matter. But I was inconsolable that day. For a small kid, the impact was huge. Over a period of years, I forgot this consciously, but my subconscious has kept it with care somewhere deep down. When I realized this reason for my aggressive behaviour, I washed out that memory from my mind. Once the effect of that memory was gone, I was totally a changed person.

Once you have decided that you want to get rid of this, the next step is how to do it. Is that a difficult or painful process? Well, it's not. And how long will it take? The answer is it can take as less as five minutes. Wow! That sounds great. So just be ready as I am now revealing this secret to you. It's very easy. In fact, it is so easy that after doing it yourself only once, you can become master of this technique and even ready to help others.

I can still recall while I was conducting a workshop in an IT company, I asked for a volunteer to come forward for the demonstration of this technique. One man came forward. To his colleagues, he was a cheerful and happy person. It looked like that he had no past issue which could trouble him. I asked him to choose an issue he wants to get rid of. Then I applied this technique to him. To the utter surprise of all, immediately tears started flowing from his eyes. He looked like the most miserable person on this earth. I changed the internal map of his pain. When I finished the exercise, he was laughing continuously. I asked him, "How much the pain of that memory is now?" He replied-which memory? It's gone now. Such is the power of this technique

The Ultimate Secret to Remove past burden

As we know that the past burden is stored in our subconscious in the form of an Internal map which may be in form of movies with audio-visual effect and we also have feelings associated with the movie. If somehow, we can change this map, automatically the feelings associated with it will change. Because feelings are relevant to that movie only.

Let's go to the root cause. We stored these burdensome events because our conscious mind had acted in that way in the past during that situation. And the subconscious as a loyal servant had stored that event the way the conscious mind had perceived. If we can consciously change the way we perceive, that means if we edit the movies the way we want for our good, things will change. This is what we will do in this powerful technique. We are now reprogramming our subconscious mind.

I'll be narrating this technique step by step. Let's start.

Step 1: Sit comfortably at a place where there is no distraction. Close your eyes and imagine that there is a thick glass wall in front of you. The glass wall is up to the ceiling height and covering the breadth of the room.

Step 2: Imagine that there is a table lying on the other side of the glass wall. Put an old television on that table. Take a pen or pencil in your hand and imagine it as the remote of the television.

Step 3: Keeping your eyes closed, switch on the television with the remote.

Step 4: Imagine the past burdensome memory in your mind. Normally, you'll find this memory in the form of movies with colours and sounds. It's also possible you have memory in a form of still pictures or in form of a movie with no colours. It may also be a black and white movie with or without the sound. Whatever it is, just follow the commands and ignore if something is not applicable.

Step 5: The remote you have in your hand is not an ordinary remote. It's a special one by which you can do whatever you want to. Now, press a button on your remote which will shift the audio-visual movie running in your mind to the screen of the television. Now you are watching this on the screen of the television.

Step 6: Next you press a button on your remote which will reduce the sound of the movie running on the television. Remember to watch the 'Yellow Stripe' on the screen. See it as decreasing to zero i.e. now the movie is mute.

Step 7: Check once again the movie on the TV for the sound. If it is mute, move to next step else repeat Step-6 until it is mute.

Step 8: Once you are assured that the movie on the TV screen is mute, it is time to dull the colours of the movie. Again, press a button on your remote and see the yellow stripe on the screen which is showing that colours are becoming dull. Keep on pressing the button until the movie is black and white.

Step 9: Once again check the movie on the TV screen for sound and colours. If the movie is mute, and black and white, go to next step else repeat previous steps till it is so.

Step 10: Now, it is time to convert all the frames of the movie to still photographs by pressing the remote button. Be ensured that there is no moving frame.

Step 11: Once again press a special button from your remote and imagine a heavy rainfall on the TV screen. The rainfall is so heavy and fast, it is dissolving all the frames of the movie and there is no remnant of any part of any frame. Keep on raining until it dissolves all the frames. Feel the water flowing under your feet.

Step 12: Check if some part of the frames is still left. Check for the corners of the screen. If still there is some trace, pour more water on it and clear everything. If still something remains, take a duster – obviously it's a magical duster – now clean the screen with the magical duster by moving quickly with your hands.

Step 13: Once all the frames are gone, it is time to say goodbye to the TV. You will press another button on the remote and you will see the television flying in the sky going towards the sun with the speed of light and turn into ashes after colliding with the sun.

Step 14: Wait! it is not yet over. Now place a big and brand-new LED television on the table. Imagine a good event which had occurred in the past. See that event running on the screen of the television in the form of a colourful movie and with sounds. Make the size of the event bigger than the life-size (at least 3-4 times bigger). Make the colours brighter and make the sounds louder – as loud as you can. Imagine your favourite music playing in the background. Press the button on your remote to transfer this beautiful memory to your mind. Feel the associated pleasant feelings. Let these feelings flow throughout your body. Enjoy these feelings for some time and then open your eyes.

Now check the intensity of your burden. If the intensity before doing this exercise was 100%, then find out what is the intensity after the exercise. You will find that the intensity has drastically decreased. Sometimes, it instantly becomes zero and people cannot recall the painful event itself. Check your intensity levels. If it is less than 50%, that means it is done. This burden has become insignificant now and not going to be a cause of trouble for you in the future. What if the intensity is over 50%? Let us say it is still 60%, 70% or more. In that case just repeat this exercise once or twice and you will get rid of the burden.

This is a simple but powerful technique. When you apply this technique to one memory, your mind will bring forward more painful memories. You need to just do the same to all of them. Once you do it for 3-4 memories, the subconscious mind will clear all the garbage as it will now consider this kind of storage useless. Hence, it will send all similar items to the trash.

Once you remove this roadblock from your mind, you will step up another stair towards your dream life.

CHAPTER 6

Secret #3: Stop being an Emotional Fool

How do you feel when someone criticizes you or scold you? Obviously, you feel bad. This is even worse if you experience such situation in presence of other persons. It affects your ego, and you feel embarrassed and ashamed. What is your response or reaction in that case? How do you handle such kind of situation?

This happens with all of us quite often. Most of us respond in two ways. One is you react right then more loudly and make the situation difficult. We see this more often in meeting rooms, at roads etc. Second is that you take it to your heart and go into shell cribbing about it. This situation is even worse. The emotions kept inside is ten times more dangerous than the emotions released. Whatever it may be, both situations are not good. Have you ever imagined what can happen in these cases? Surely, you'd have but not at the time of handling the situation. If you fight with someone, this may even harm you physically; no surprise you hear so many road rage deaths. If you retaliate in front of your boss, you can even lose your job.

I myself was a victim of these reactions. As I had mentioned earlier that because of the insecurity complex, I used to shout a lot on others whenever I felt I have been criticized. In fact, when people react to their circumstances, they more likely suffer from this insecurity complex. Their reaction is to hide this insecurity from the world. Same was happening to me. Even when a person was saying it for my benefit, I used to show outbursts. I suffered a lot because of this.

I would like to narrate an incident which helped me to change the way I used to think. I was working with a reputed organization and my responsibility was to ensure material for the project team. There were issues related to material which the project team had escalated to the Managing Director. He called our team for an urgent meeting along with other stakeholders. I knew the issue pertains to poor forecasts that have resulted in this problem. The Managing Director scolded the whole team in a high pitch. I felt terrible and tried to narrate the story behind this issue which made the situation even worse. This hurt my ego, and I started shouting in the loud tone. You would have imagined what happened next? Yes, you are right. MD immediately ordered me to put the papers, and in the heat of the moment, I also sent the resignation mail.

At the end, who lost? It was me only. I was without a job with millions of loans on my head. Had I thought this before I retaliated, I would not have done this. This is what we all need to do. If we think what the outcome of my behaving in this way could be, we can avoid many unpleasant events by choosing our behaviour.

Now, I was without a job. My colleagues advised me to go to MD and say sorry to him. I took his appointment. When I met him and apologized, within a few minutes everything was set right. He advised me to work on my behaviour. I took it in a positive spirit and started meditating daily. I used to meditate for two hours a day. Within a few months, I was getting results. My behaviour got changed. This was the time I learned various techniques to manage myself. By the end of next year, I was a changed person. Not only at the office, my relationships with my family, friends, and colleagues also got strengthened. This was now helping me in all spheres of life.

You must be thinking it is difficult to stay calm when someone is behaving harshly. I agree with you, but what it will give you when you also behave in the same manner. Relationships break mostly because of this reason only. Just develop 'So What' attitude. This is a powerful method if you use it properly. Here I am not saying you shirk your responsibilities by saying this to yourself. I am only asking you to keep these emotions outside and not letting in your mind and heart. Just get them off your mind. Seems difficult. Try it.

Apart from this, there is a master technique to protect yourself from the verbal attacks. I apply this technique quite often. This is a wonderful technique. It has worked for me and I am sure will work for you also. Earlier I used to have many heated confrontations with my boss – almost daily. Then I applied this beautiful technique. This is such a powerful technique I enjoyed a much better relation with my boss once I applied this.

I taught this technique to my younger son as he used to complain about his elder brother. His complaint was that the big brother teased him by saying things which he did not like. You know, this happens with brothers. So I told him that whenever brother says something you do not want to hear, imagine yourself in a transparent bubble. So you can also do the same. Just imagine that you are in a big transparent bubble. The bubble is so big that you can do whatever you want to do in it. There is plenty of air in the bubble so that you don't feel suffocated. You may imagine that the bubble is extremely strong and unbreakable by anything in this universe. You can also imagine that your God, Guru or Deity is giving blessings to this bubble to provide more strength. Whenever any person is saying something to you by which you feel hurt, just imagine that their words are travelling from their mouth to the bubble and after striking the bubble (bubble is very strong and unbreakable) and unable to penetrate, they are falling down. When these words fall down, see them falling on the ground and breaking into pieces. Listen the sound also at this time. You can imagine, some words are going back to the mouth of the person. If a person is standing behind you and trying to hurt you, even then these words cannot penetrate the bubble. Wherever the person is, you are safe in the bubble and no emotional garbage can enter inside. Practice this, and in a few days, you'll find the difference.

Now, there is one flaw in this method. If a person is saying something for your benefit and his tone is harsh, your bubble will not let it enter. So, what to do in that case. There is a remedy to this. You imagine a wisdom window in that bubble which will open when such a situation occurs. It is an automatic window and will open itself. You need not do any effort to open this. Just create this window and forget. It'll work on its own. This way the communication which is for your benefit will reach you even if the tone of the person is not up to the mark. This is a marvellous technique and does wonders.

There is one more master technique, which helped me in managing my emotions. The bubble technique which I have told you is to be used in 'LIVE' condition. This technique which I will tell you now, is a preventive technique and you'll do it at your home or at any place where distractions are minimum.

To start with, just find a comfortable place at your home where you can lie down. Be sure that there are no distractions around. Be ready to get started. Lie down on your back leaving some space between the feet. Your palms should face upwards.

Just relax yourself by taking three-four deep breaths. Now scan your body from your toe to your head. Imagine as if you are outside your body and seeing each part of your body. Start from the toes and then move to ankles, legs, knees, thighs and lower part of your stomach. While scanning, feel the heaviness of the flesh and bones in your body. This represents the earth element of this universe. Imagine that the earth element outside and inside your body is one and same. Keep moving from the lower part of the stomach to upwards, and try to see the organs inside your body – kidneys, pancreas, lungs, intestine etc. Keep moving up feeling the heaviness of flesh and bones. See your lower back, spine, upper back, upper abdominal area, chest, heart, neck, both hands, fingers, shoulders. Keep moving upwards to chin, cheeks, lips, nose, eyes, eyelids, forehead and go to the crown. This way you are scanning your whole body and connecting it to the earth element of this universe.

Now, take a couple of deep breaths, and feel the flow of blood in your veins and arteries. This blood represents the water element of this universe. Once again, imagine that the water element outside and inside is same. Spend some time doing this.

Next, you feel the warmth in your whole body. This warmness represents the fire element of the universe and again imagine that fire element outside and inside is one and same. Enjoy for some time before moving to the next step.

After this, you examine the space inside your body where there is no muscle, bone or vein. There is absolutely nothing. This represents the ether element of the universe.

Once you are done, just focus your attention on your breath. Just observe your breath. Don't try to change its pace. Just observe calmly. This is nothing but the air element of this universe. Feel the oneness with all the elements of this universe.

Enjoy this for some more time. Post this, imagine that a white or golden colour celestial light is entering your body through your navel and it is flowing throughout your body. Visualize your body is filled with white/ golden light. Imagine yourself surrendering to this white/ golden light. Feel you are melting in this powerful magical light and a new 'You' is emerging out of this. This 'You' is very powerful and magnificent and is what you have been imagining yourself in your dreams. Whatever good feelings you are having at this moment, multiply them many folds and let it flow to each and every cell of your body. Let the entire world know a new 'YOU' has arrived.

Keep lying in that position for some more time enjoying these feelings. Then, slowly move your fingers, move your legs, rub your palms and put it on your face. Now, slowly open your eyes.

This is the technique which was primarily responsible to change my life. Not only did I become happy and healthier, but I also converted into a much more energetic and positive person.

Now that you have shed your past burden and learnt to handle your emotions effectively, you have made your foundation very strong. Now it is time to make a beautiful palace on such a strong foundation. In the next section, you will learn to create a zone of excellence for yourself.

C

Create Your Zone of Excellence

CHAPTER 7

Secret #4: Make Yourself Bigger than the Problems

We all need a life full of happiness, prosperity, health, and success without any problem. What do you think, is that possible? Can we have a life with no problem at all? Well, we all know the answer. Problems will be there as long as we live. I'd like to correct this sentence. Instead of problems, I call them stimuli which tries to enter our mind to get converted into problems. Who converts them into problems? None other than our mind.

I want you to introspect yourself right now. What is the relative size of your problems? How do you deal with them? When clients come to me, they behave in different ways as far as their body language is concerned. They indicate with their hand (by expanding) to point out the size of their problem. Some of them expand it making a big circle outside their body – a circle bigger than themselves. This shows that their problems are much bigger than their own self. There is another type of people who enclose themselves into the problem which is even more dangerous thing. Here not only the size of the problem is huge but also, they are into it. This situation creates suicidal tendencies in the person. I want you to find out the size of your problems. If it is much less than your own self, then probably you don't need this technique. But most of us have a distorted self-image so much that every problem seems to be a monster. So, just check out in which category do you fit in? Size of your problem is less than yourself or it is bigger, or you are enclosed into it.

As long as our problems remain gigantic, we cannot cross the barrier encircled by these beasts. So, what should we do? During my childhood, I had learnt a trick to make a line drawn on the slate short. You all remember the trick. Aren't you? The best way to make that line short was to draw another line bigger than it. This is what we will do here. Problems are the stimuli which can act as a stressor only if we allow it to do so. We allow them to become problems because we have a low and distorted self-image. If we perceive these stimuli in such a way that they look very tiny to us, then the job is done. This is possible if we magnify our self-image to that extent that all the stimuli become minuscule. When our self-image is low, we crib to circumstances outside rather than take charge of the situation. This is the difference between successful and unsuccessful people. The low self-image will decrease the confidence level and creates self-doubt which creates the fear. Once this fear overtakes you, you lose the battle even before starting.

We have been distorting our self-image for such a long time that we ourselves have forgotten who we are. We don't know ourselves. Let us do a reality check. I ask you to just close your eyes and see the face of a person whom you think is a big celebrity. See that person closely and analyze the images you are getting on your mental screen for a few seconds. Now open your eyes. How was the image? Most of you would have a clear, colourful image (some may see in form of a movie as well), closer to your mind screen, bigger in the size. Now, repeat this with your image. Yes, you heard it right. Try to see your image on your mental screen for a few seconds now. You'd yourself see the difference between the quality of the two images. Many of my clients cannot even see their image and most of the remaining have blurred image, smaller in size, and at a distance from their mental screen, opposite to what they see for their celebrity. We have such a spectacular image of our celebrity but not ours. If this is the case with you also, you'll be full of anxiety, get irritated frequently and perceive the goals as a burden. In such a scenario, achieving the desired results will look impossible to you.

Therefore, if you want to get the life you dream, you need to build a strong self-image. I will explain an incredible technique to improve your self-image.

Close your eyes and imagine any instance from your life (past or recent) when you were lacking your self-esteem. Visualize those scenarios on your mental screen as if it is happening now. Make a note of all the pictures/ movies, sounds, feelings etc. in your mind. Now shift your attention from this event. Spell your name in the reverse direction. (this is just to break the state).

Create your image in front of the mental screen such that it is at some distance from you. Imagine this image is a live person who is representing yourself in the future. This 'Future You' has already solved all the problems which affect your self-image. Imagine this 'Future You' achieving all the goals which you have set for your dream life. The 'Future You' knows you would succeed because this 'You' has already succeeded.

See this 'Future You' in front of you and make a large and colourful image of this 'You', having all the resources needed to handle all kinds of issues. The 'Future You' has all the traits you wished for. This 'You' is happy, confident, full of energy, healthy, motivated and a winner. Imagine the people significant to you are appreciating this 'You' for achieving what you had strived for. Make the images brighter and bolder, and two to three times larger than the life-size. Make these images as attractive as you can.

Now see the attractive 'Future You' is talking confidently in a powerful voice. Imagine this 'You' is saying that "I feel worthy about myself", "I feel great about myself". Imagine that this image is now converted into a golden ball and this ball is floating in front of you.

Imagine what other traits this 'Future You' should have. It can be to accept criticism with positivity, humour, listening skills, flexibility, love etc. you can choose whatever you want to.

Now imagine that the golden ball has expanded again and you can see the healthy, happy, energetic, motivated and a winner 'Future You' in front of you. Now add more traits to this 'You' which you want to. See this 'You' displaying all these characteristics. Make all the images bigger, bolder and brighter.

Once again, shrink this 'Future You' into a tiny golden ball. Now imagine that this golden ball has converted itself into billions of similar golden balls. Now imagine your self-image which you had imagined at the start of this exercise. Think of a machine in which these billions of golden balls are placed, and this machine will throw the balls at your command.

Give a command to this machine to throw a golden ball to your mental screen where your old self-image is placed. The moment this golden ball strikes your mental screen, it tears the old image into pieces; the golden ball expands, and all the images of the golden ball take the place of the old image. This happens almost instantly. The time between striking the ball on your mental screen and expansion of all the images of the ball should not be over 2-3 seconds.

Now Imagine that the speed of the machine is increasing, and it is throwing the balls at a much faster pace now. In a moment you see that all the billions of balls are striking on your mental screen at once and the billions of images are getting displayed on your mental screen completely omitting the old image. you are integrating this new and powerful image with yourself. Let these powerful feelings flow throughout your body. Intensify these feelings. Enjoy them for some time before opening your eyes.

Do this at least 30 times at once to get better results. Post that, see your image on the mental screen. You will find a new and better image in place of the old image. With this exercise, you have started creating the patterns of positivity and opportunities for yourself. Let us now learn how to always be in such a state where we always enjoy these patterns.

CHAPTER 8

Secret #5: Learn to be in Groove

We have learnt how our mind creates the state and how this makes us behave in a way to create our destiny. That means if I can learn a technique by which I remain in a resourceful state of mind, then my behaviours and actions will change in my favour thus creating a destiny which I desire.

When Ashutosh, a top management official working in a multinational company came to me, he was undergoing a rough phase in his career. His career was at stake. He was in his unresourceful (or stuck) state, not able to think what he should do to set everything right.

When you are in a stuck state, you are in a state of stress, anxiety, and fear. In such a state, you miss out even the opportunities because of lack of access to your own resources. That means you cannot use your own potential. You cannot see them as opportunities since you are in a firefighting mode. This way you may convert opportunities into crisis and feel left behind in the race of life. Moreover, you may suffer in terms of health, finances, relationships, peace of mind and what not. When you are in such a state, you procrastinate the things and create doubt on your own self and this further lowers your self-esteem.

All this was happening with Ashutosh and he wanted a fast relief. I understood his problem and could make out immediately that he needs to correct his state immediately. I knew he'll be all right once he gets his resourceful state as he had all the skills to handle the situation.

Most often, people think resourceful state is something which a handful of fortunate people only enjoy while others are just praying to have it. This is not correct. This state is not a thing which you get through your genes and you cannot create. Instead, it results from the way our mind perceives things. When mind perceives failures, we feel low and our confidence takes a hit. At that time, our body releases stress hormones predominantly adrenalin and cortisol. So, is there anything we can do to boost our confidence at our own will? What if we can learn how to be in our resourceful state – a state full of confidence and energy- so that our body releases positive chemicals dopamine, oxytocin, testosterone, serotonin etc. and we are in a state of high confidence?

We can learn it consciously and be in our the most confident state all the time. We can achieve this by reprogramming our mind or correcting our physiology. As we know both the mind and body are connected i.e. our thoughts affect our mind and vice versa. As the mind changes, our body changes and the same way reverse is also true. Change in one will influence the other.

If you want to make yourself productive, achieve your goals, fulfil your dreams and get what you desire, you need to have a resourceful state of mind. This way you gain greater inner strength, happiness, and power to stand up after failures.

You will now learn scientific and unique techniques which you can easily follow and implement. I will not give something from the outside world that'll improve your state. It's there inside you only. I am just going to help you tap your own resources. Yeah, you heard it right. It's already within you. So, here is the first technique.

Correcting Physiology

First thing I told Ashutosh is to correct his physiology. As we now know a change in our mind has a corresponding change in our body and vice versa. When we are in an unresourceful state of mind, it is reflected in our physiology. If you see a person who is nervous, depressed or stressed, watch his physiology. He will look downwards most of the time. He will have drooping or sagging shoulders. You can see all sorts of negativity on the face of such a person.

So, if we change something in our body which can change the state of our mind, then the job is done. And luckily, we can do this. We can correct our physiology so that hormones such as testosterone, oxytocin, dopamine flow in our body and mood depressing hormones like cortisol decreases to reduce our anxiety and nervousness. This will help us in dealing with situations in a better way. That means we can change our physiology such that a signal goes to our mind to bring us in a resourceful and confident state. Now, the question is how to do it? What is that posture which brings us in such a state?

Well, that's what I will reveal now. And the amazing thing is that this works almost instantaneously. This is what I told Ashutosh to do immediately. This technique works like a first aid. I asked him to stand straight with spine erect and shoulders upright. Then I told him to close his eyes and just scan his body form the toes of feet till the crown of the head. His body language changed immediately. Then, I told him to take a few deep breaths and imagine that with every 'breathe in' he is inhaling positive energy flowing throughout your body. Likewise, with every 'breathe out' imagine that all the negativity is getting out of the body and mind. I asked him to bring a broad smile on his face imagining any moment of happiness from your past.

Ashutosh was feeling better. Then I said, Ashutosh! Open your eyes and look upwards and keep doing so for at least 2-3 minutes. He immediately said, "Wow! What a wonderful technique, I am feeling better."

This is such a wonderful technique and yet so simple you can do it anywhere. Whenever you have something important coming up like an exam, job interview, presentation etc. which has potential to make you anxious or feel low, just do this for two minutes before the start of your assignment. Obviously, you may not do it before interviewer or in the boardroom. In such a case, you may do it in the washroom or at such a place where no one is around. I have done this even at the parking. Believe me, this does the wonders.

Apart from this, inculcate a habit to do this for some time at home every morning. This will help you in keeping your spirits up throughout the day.

Ashutosh was now feeling good. He had tasted the blood now. He said, "Nilesh, I need more". I said, "Tell me, what do you want?" He then said I have a job interview planned tomorrow. I need to crack this interview. I asked him to do the same what I had just taught him. Apart from that, I gave him another master technique to create the zone of excellence. Now, I will unearth this technique to you. It will help you all the time throughout your life. You may call this technique as Circle of Excellence.

Circle of Excellence

Choose a comfortable place where you have no distractions. Stand up with your spine straight and shoulders upright as if you are confident. Close your eyes. Create an internal sound-"My name is……. (your name) and I am confident." Bring the expressions of confidence on your face.

Now Imagine a situation in your life when you enjoyed confidence. You can even think of a small situation when you had answered a question confidently or showed someone a correct way to reach one's destination. Once you recall that incident when you were confident, watch it in form of a movie in front of your mental screen. See the colours of the movie, listen the sounds in the movie and experience the feelings you were enjoying at that time. Make the pictures bigger, brighter and bolder now; make the volume of sounds louder and intensify the feelings.

As you enjoy the peak of feelings of confidence keeping your spine straight and shoulders upright, imagine a circle around your feet. In this circle imagine a colour matching with the feelings of confidence. Imagine that blessings of your God/Guru/Deity in the form of white light is falling in this circle. Imagine a sound like 'WOW' in this circle.

Now, imagine that this colour with the WOW sound is entering your body through your feet and mixing with the feelings of confidence you are enjoying. Imagine this colour mixed with feelings and sound is flowing throughout your body. After this, you leave these colourful feelings and sound back into the circle and step back to get out of the circle. Open your eyes. Look around and once again close your eyes.

Imaging a future event where you want to enjoy these feelings of confidence This event can be your exam, interview, performing on stage, giving presentation etc. Visualize how you want to perform at that event. Imagine what benefits you will be enjoying in short-term and long-term. Once you are clear of your outcome what you want, enter the circle again. Keep your spine straight, shoulders upright, and imagine taking all the feelings of confidence mixed with colours and sound, from the circle in your mind and body. Enjoy the peak of your confidence. Now enter the desired situation in future and live it the way you want to. Watch the movie of your desired outcome running in front you. Make the pictures in the movie more colourful, bigger and bolder. Increase the volume of sounds and intensify the feelings. See you achieving your desired results and people are appreciating you for this achievement. Remember to see your significant people in the movie appreciating you and congratulating you. Once it is done, leave all the feelings mixed with colour into the circle again and step back to get out of the circle.

Repeat this exercise at least 20 times to get the desired results. First time you may do it slower. But subsequently, you must do it very fast – as fast as possible.

Once Ashutosh did this technique, he was in the other world. He went home satisfied and happy. Next day he called me up to thank me for giving him such a wonderful technique. He said his interview went well; much better than his expectations.

There is another simple technique you can use to remain in the groove. This technique is called 'As If' technique wherein you imagine that you have achieved the resourceful state of mind. It is a kind of self-suggestion. I am giving you command of this technique now.

As If

It is the simplest and one of the most powerful technique. You need to just imagine that you are confident. You say to yourself aloud (in your mind) and imagine yourself behaving as if you are confident. You not only imagine but also act as if you are confident. That means "Fake it till you Make it". You continue to do it until this happens. First, stand up and keep your spine straight and shoulders upright. This is a powerful position keeping the energy flow to the maximum. Now, say in your mind as if I am confident. Say it loudly; as loudly as possible but in your mind only. While you are saying it in your mind, see yourself in your mind doing things with the confidence which you normally think you cannot do. Try to see yourself with a lot of clarity. Do not expect this technique to give instant results. This takes time. Combine this technique with the first one i.e. correcting physiology to get the maximum benefit.

With this, you have learnt to create your zone of excellence in your internal world. Next, we will learn how to do it in external world.

CHAPTER 9

Secret #6: Create a Magical Bond

A salesperson works very hard, gives beautiful presentations but cannot convert into sales. But his colleague in lesser time and with lesser efforts can do.

A parent is asking his children to behave in a particular fashion or to do something, and they are not even listening.

Husband and wife who had the love marriage, now have an issue with each and are not enjoying their relationships as they were earlier.

A speaker is holding a seminar and most of the people are set off.

Does something sound common to you? Well, I guess, we all go through these or similar issues when we try to communicate with others and don't get the desired result.

And we say the other person is not listening. Is there a problem with other persons or are we not communicating the language they understand? All the cases which I mentioned above are the cases of non-establishment of rapport.

We live in such a society we need to communicate properly with so many people to fulfill our needs. These people may be colleagues or boss at the office, spouse or kids at home, friends, relatives or even unknown people. It's therefore essential for us to create a rapport with them. Creating rapport does not mean that the other person will agree or will get convinced. It may be possible you may not have established the rapport with a person, but you agree with the person. A classic example may be your Boss. Similarly, you may be in rapport with your spouse but disagree on some issue. The rapport and agreement are hence two different things. Rapport means that a person is now willing to understand other's point of view.

Once you are in rapport with others, you can build satisfying relationships. Then, other persons will be happily supporting you in achieving your goals.

At the start of this chapter, I mentioned that a couple have issues with each other. Wife complains that her hubby does not care about her. While the husband says, we had a foreign tour few months back; last month only I have gifted her a very expensive dress. We go to dinner often. What else should I do? The wife replies all these things are OK but when was the last time he said, "I Love You".

Are you getting a hint here, the husband has done so many things for his wife, still she is not happy? What do you think is the gap here?

Husband is not doing what his wife wants. That's it. That means both are on the different platform. Husband is trying to show while wife wants to hear. The gap is in the representational system they are using. Oh! I have not told you about the preferred representational system yet. Let me do it first.

Preferred Representational System

As we know, we perceive using five senses. Out of these five senses, we normally use three senses while communicating. These are visual sense, auditory sense, and kinesthetic (feeling) sense. We have learnt in the first part of this book how we perceive things and creates an internal map in our mind. This internal map has a subjective event in the form of visual, auditory and kinesthetic. It is not always necessary that the map has an equal proportion of these three. It may be in any proportion, in fact it may be possible that for an event one or two of these are missing or are in meagre proportion. This way a person may store events in visual dominant or auditory dominant or in kinesthetic dominant representation. Thus, some people prefer to perceive things in images, some in sounds and some in feelings. This is their preferred representational system. Hence there are three preferred representational system – Visual, Auditory and Kinesthetic.

If we need to establish rapport, we need to communicate with the other persons as per their preferred representational system. This way we can enter their world and establish rapport. Thus, rapport is a bonding at the subconscious level. Why is this effective? Because we like similarities. This is the human tendency to prefer people whom our mind perceives as similar. When we use the representational system which the other person is using, we perceive that the person is like us and hence we can establish rapport.

Identifying People with Different Representational System

In the case of the couple, the husband was communicating using his visual representational system to his auditory wife. This was the only gap. Had he known this, he would have done the correct thing. Now the question arises how to identify the preferred representational system of a person. It is not that difficult. We can do it by checking physiology. Just check the eye movement, voice, breathing pattern, postures and gestures to know what kind of representational system, a person is using. Preferred does not mean that the person will use only that representational system. It means that most of the time, the person uses the preferred one. A person with a visual preferred representational system may use other systems in some other situation.

Visual persons use visualization for the communication. They see the things in form of movies. If you see them, they mostly look upwards (specifically left up when they remember something and right up when they create some new images). You may think they are not looking at you and paying attention, but actually, they are watching their movies and if someone interrupts them, they may lose their movie altogether and forget what they were talking. Hence, never interrupt a visual person. Sometimes, they may look straight also but they are not looking at you instead they will be defocused and busy watching their movies. If you see their hands, they draw something in the air. While speaking you can see the tension in their body. You can even see their breathing as high and shallow. Visual people speak fast, and their tone is high. While communicating to such persons, ensure that you are using their language. Use pictures and movies to explain things to such a person and never ever interrupt them as this can end the communication. Selection of words should also be the same which they are using such as visualize, imagine, focus, see, show, highlight, watch outlook, preview, etc.

Auditory people love to hear, especially their own voice. They look down on their left while doing so. When they hear some known things outside, their eyes go towards the left ear and when they listen to some new things their eye movement is towards the right ear. They tilt their head to one side and their movement is rhythmic. If you analyze their tone, it will be melodious with normal pace and pauses. They breathe at a normal pace – neither too slow nor too fast. When you find someone whom you are communicating with as an auditory person, use their preferred representational system. You may use words such as hear, listen, talk, noise, tell, loud, audible, discuss, tone, musical, echo, etc.

Likewise, kinesthetic people also show cues. They like to look down on their right side while communicating. They have a low and deep tone, and take long pauses. They talk slowly and while communicating their muscles are relaxed. Their breathing will be deep. There is one special thing that while communicating, they like to touch the other person or things placed nearby and if they don't find anything else, they touch themselves. They use words like feel, touch, smell, hold, grasp, handle, rough, warm, cool, etc.

It's that simple. Just identify the representational system the other person is using and step into the same representational system consciously. Once you do this, you are now in rapport with the other person. If you recall the case of husband and wife, their problem is a classic case of miscommunication because of the usage of different representational systems. Here, the husband loves his wife, and he is giving her expensive dress and taking her on a foreign tour. He wants to make his wife happy. But the problem is that husband is using the visual representational system while the wife is using auditory. Wife only wants to hear. Had the husband known this, it would have saved him a lot of money in buying the expensive dress and on the foreign tour. Hahaha!

If the case is between people where one is visual and the other is kinesthetic. Well, it can be a disaster. Visual and kinesthetic people do not see each other eye to eye. Visual likes to do things fast while kinesthetic is slow. The gap between these two is huge. Kinesthetic would like to touch while speaking which visual hates at all. So, if two persons are communicating; one using visual and other using kinesthetic representational system, then it will be a complete mess.

Now, imagine a salesperson has a specific target to sell a product. He will have different clients and they may use different representational system. Suppose one of the clients is visual. If the salesperson keeps on telling stories about the product, it will turn off the visual. Instead, what he needs to do is to show the product, show fancy presentations about the product. And then give him some time to create his movie or image in the mind. The salesman needs to use the hands freely while discussing as it will help the client to make a clear picture in the mind. If he can make pictures, he will immediately decide.

This method will not work if your client is auditory. Here, the best way is to tell about your product and, if possible, tell about the auditory properties of your product. For example, if you are selling a machine, you may mention about the sound of the machine. Use musical or rhythmic words in your discussion. In many cases, light soothing background music also helps. But do not keep on talking continuously. Just tell him about the product and then give your client a chance to talk to himself and to you. Auditory people like to take a decision based on what they hear inside. The best salesman for him is his own voice. Carefully listen to him as while talking he is likely to give you a clue how to close the deal. Never ever give them multiple choices as they won't be able to conclude. Don't force them to decide immediately. Once you are done with the meeting, follow up with a telephone call.

Selling a product to a kinesthetic client is both easy and difficult. Because it all depends on the mood of the client. If the person is in a good mood, chances of closing the deal are bright. But if he has a fight with his wife in the morning, you are gone. So, if you see the mood of your kinesthetic client is off, the best strategy is to avoid discussing with him. Just say hello and take the next appointment. When you meet a kinesthetic client in a normal or good mood, do not waste time in showing presentations or telling stories. Give him a feel of your product or if you want to show presentations, these should be emotionally charged ones as your client will respond better. Such clients usually take decisions on their gut feelings. So, give him things to touch to create feelings. This way you can better your chance of sales.

Mirroring Physiology

Apart from this, you can also build rapport by mirroring the physiology of the other person. You can mirror the body language, gestures, postures, expressions, etc. If you are communicating with a person and he has his right leg on his left leg, you may mirror him by putting your left leg on your right leg. Now suppose he changes his posture and sits straight with crossed fingers. You won't do it immediately as he might notice it, and this will put you in an awkward situation. Just count from one to ten in your mind and swiftly change your position to mirror him. When you do this, a communication goes to his subconscious mind that you are like him. This establishes the rapport between you and him. Now pacing is complete. Once pacing is complete, and the rapport is established, if you change your posture, you will see the other person will also mirror you. This stage is called leading. Now you have better chances to influence the other person. This can be difficult in starting but with practice, you may master this art of mirroring. If you analyze, you are regularly doing this technique unconsciously while talking to your near and dear ones.

Whenever you are communicating with a person, take a genuine interest in what the other person is saying. Try to maintain curiosity by asking relevant questions. It's always better to lean slightly forward as this will send a signal that you understand the other person's point of view. This way you can create a strong bond with the person.

So far, we have discussed the case of one-to-one communication. What if you need to communicate with a group or maybe you need to address a large gathering?

There may be persons with different representational systems. If you use a sentence – "I want to show this", this will attract only visuals and others will not be interested. Likewise, "I want to tell you something" will cater to the auditory population only while "I smell something wrong" will address kinesthetic people. So, what to do here. Here we need to create an impact on all of them at once. You will find writers and poets use words which impact all kinds of people. So, use such sentences which everyone can appreciate i.e. your speech should have visual, auditory and kinesthetic words. One such example may be "When golden rays from the Sun touches your face, thousands of violins start playing in my heart." This is just an example. I am not asking you to be romantic in your speech. Just try practicing using words of different representational systems in your sentences and after practice, it will come to you naturally.

If you learn to create a rapport with the different persons, your relationships will be better. Relationships play an important role in the life be it at home or office or anywhere. When relationships are better, one can get support from the people and hence move towards our goals in a faster and smoother way. Now you have learnt how to create the zone of excellence for yourself, we are left with another powerful technique wherein you will find out the misalignment among your neurological levels. Until you align all these levels, you cannot reach your destination.

CHAPTER 10

Secret #7: Align your Neurological Levels

Imagine you are going to a car showroom to buy a car. Salesman shows you the car and tells that every part of the car is the best in the world. You take a test drive only to find that there is a small issue with the car. When you turn to the right side, it moves backward; when you apply brakes, it speeds up; and when you try to take a right turn it stops. Though all the parts are brand new and the best in class but the alignment between the parts is missing. Will you buy such a car? Obviously not. In the similar way, though you have made the master plan, cleared all the objections and started your journey towards your wonderful dream life, still there may be something which can pull you back. All of us operate at different levels which we call Neurological Levels. If there is misalignment among these levels, the life will be like the car in which different parts are not in congruence with each other. Robert Dilts has mentioned these neurological levels as:

1. Environment
2. Behaviours
3. Skills/Capabilities
4. Beliefs and Values
5. Identity
6. Spiritual

These levels can be bifurcated into two zones. The three levels from environment to skills, make one zone which we call as reactive zone while the other levels belong to the active zone.

If we apply these levels to the life as a whole, the alignment among these levels is a must, to realize the dreams. Normally it should happen that our behaviours and actions should have been driven by or in accordance with our beliefs, values, identity and the purpose of life. But if we see in our lives, our behaviours are not aligned with any of these levels. This is the real cause of sorrows. Imagine a person who has a belief about money that "money is just like dirt on your hands", he does not value money and his identity is still that of a middle-class person, do you think he'll be able to excel as far as money is concerned. Similarly, if a child has a belief, that studies are useless, he values social media more than studies and he has made his identity as a social media visitor, will he be able to excel in the studies? The answers are quite obvious. That is why this alignment is very critical to achieve success in life. Once we correct this misalignment, we can move smoothly in life with no hiccups.

Let us understand what these levels are.

1. **Environment** is the surroundings where you operate. It includes people and places around you. In your environment, you do certain things just to please others and don't do certain things not to displease others
2. **Behaviours** are nothing but the actions you take in the environment. It includes your movements, postures etc. You may imagine a typical day to take a note of your behaviours.
3. **Skills and capabilities** are your internal resources which you use to deal with different circumstances.
4. **Beliefs** are what you think it can happen or not. It's basically your faith and trust based on the perception of your mind. Imagine there is a person who has issues with his relations and wants to improve it. On asking about his beliefs about relations, he says the relationship is a trap. Will he ever be having a good relationship? You know how to get out of a trap. One can come out of a trap

only by cutting it. So, if he will also come out of the relationship by ruining it.

Beliefs are formed because of our subjective experience of events. As we know that we store subjective experience of an event in our mind after deletion, distortion, and generalization. These experiences act as a reference for our mind. But they are not converted into beliefs immediately. When we have similar experiences, again and again, these get converted into beliefs. Hence, beliefs are nothing but reinforced subjective experiences.

"Beliefs are the reinforced subjective experiences of our mind."

—Nilesh Goswami

Beliefs can also be formed when a person significant to you tells you something, especially when you are a child. A child takes the information as such, without deletion, distortion, and generalization because it has been told by a person significant to him. That is why we make most of our beliefs based on what our parents and teachers say to us because they are the significant persons in our life. If our parents have told us during our young age that money is just a dirt on hand; it spoils relationship and brings evil along with it. In whatever sense or mood, it has been said, our subconscious mind takes it as a belief as our logical mind is not yet developed fully during that stage. The logical mind is fully developed only by the age of nine years. If we have such kind of belief about money, then we cannot earn money in life. Because the subconscious mind who is a storehouse and an alarm indicator will keep on sending alarms to us regarding money. Such kinds of beliefs are limiting beliefs. We can have similar limiting beliefs about health, career, success, relationships, etc. These beliefs stop us from moving ahead in life towards the success. We need to replace these beliefs by opposite beliefs. Now the question is how to replace these limiting beliefs? The answer lies in the secret how did we create them. These beliefs were created by the subconscious mind based on the experience of conscious mind. We can break them in the same way. We can consciously send information and experience, which is opposite to the limiting beliefs to the subconscious mind continuously. The subconscious mind will take that because it is a loyal storekeeper and takes the experiences and feelings of the conscious mind as such. By feeding with such feelings continuously, the subconscious mind will accept new empowered beliefs and abandon the old ones.

V**alues** are nothing but what you feel important for you. Suppose the man in above example, says his values are freedom and commitment. Here, because of commitment, he will enter into a relationship. He enjoys it for some time until the other value stands in front of him. Then he will say oh my God I have lost my freedom. As a result, he will come out of the relationship for his freedom. After some time once again, his earlier value will appear in front of him and he will again go into a relationship only to get out because of other value- freedom. What's happening here? He has two values which are contradictory, and he has not set the hierarchy of the values. So, when these two contradictory values come in front of him, he gets confused which value to choose. Similarly, if a person has two conflicting values wherein he wants to get success and he does not want to get rejected. You know both things are not possible. Whatever you do there will be people who will be criticizing you. It is not possible that hundred percent people appreciate you. So, when you do something, sometimes you may fail also. If you have these two values, until you are getting success you are all right, but the day you fail – even if you fail once in a hundred times- you will get demotivated, and it is possible you leave that thing and start other. It is also possible you may not even start a work because of fear of getting rejected. What you need to do is to clear the hierarchy of your values. The task is simple. You list down a number of things important for you in life i.e. you are listing down all of your values. If the list is very big, write at least ten values. Next job is to rank these values, so you know which value has priority over other values. This will help you in taking a decision in case of conflicts. Do it right now before moving further.

5. **Identity** is the level of your self-image. It also means, with what do you identify yourself? How worthy do you think of yourself?

   Here I ask myself who am I? Am I Nilesh Goswami? But that is just a name given by my parents. Am I a life coach? That is my professional identity. Am I a father, son, husband or brother? Well, that is my social identity. Do I belong to or support a political party? That is my political identity. Then who am I? I like you to ask this question today. Who are you? I tell you who are you. Whenever you use a word after 'I am' repeatedly, you create that identity in your subconscious mind and the mind programs you to become that. For example, if you say I am depressed and say it repeatedly, your subconscious mind will make all the arrangements to make you depressed. After all, it is a loyal servant to the conscious mind. Same goes for when you say I am cheated; I am diabetic; I am a fool; I am stupid etc. etc. So, in the future watch out what you are using after "I am" as you are creating your identity. If you keep on making your middle-class identity or identity of a victim, I am sorry to say whatever technique you may use, it will be a waste. Create a strong identity for yourself which will take you towards your dreams.

6. **Spiritual level** is basically the bigger purpose of your life. Let us not confuse this spiritual level with attaining 'Moksha'. Here the context is life i.e. how to achieve the dream goals which we desire in this life. So, we will restrict ourselves to that only. This is the topmost level where you find what for you have been senton this earth. We will discuss more on this level when we will do the exercise.

Get ready to walk on these levels. I will implant all these things right now so that you get your alignment of all the levels correct. That too right now. Get ready for this powerful exercise. Find out a place where no one distracts you. You need to walk six steps so there should be sufficient space for you to do this exercise. We'll first go from the level of the environment to the highest level and then come back.

Imagine that you are at the level of your environment. Just see what kind of environment you have. Do not evaluate anything now. It may be good or bad whatever it is, just check the quality of your environment.

Now take a step back and reach the level of your behaviours. Here again, check the quality of your behaviours. Imagine your typical day and visualize how do you behave or what are your actions in different situations and with different people. Sometimes, you will find your behaviours are all right but sometimes you may find some shocking or surprising behaviours. Without analyzing take one step back.

You are now at the level of your skills and capabilities. See what percentage of your skills you are using in day-to-day life. You will find that sometimes you are doing wonderful but sometimes you are not using your skills properly where you could have used it.

These three levels belong to the reactive zone. Ordinary people work at this level. They focus on improving the environment, building more skills and improving their behaviours. Not that skills are not important. But if you are at some level in your life, you do have the skills. You can find several examples of extraordinary people who did not have a proper environment, but they never cursed their environment or circumstances. If you take the example of Abraham Lincoln or Dr. APJ Kalam, they did not have the environment which many of us have been enjoying since childhood. You can focus on changing behaviours but how many of us get successful? If I tell you to get up at 4 am from tomorrow or you come in time from the very next day, will you start doing it from the day one? Obviously not. You may appreciate that it is good to do these things and even want to do but you simply cannot do. Reason you know. Behaviours are not the root cause, instead they are the product of our state which is created by our internal map. So, the change is required at the subconscious level, not at the behavioural level. In fact, you may find many people whose behaviours are less polished than yours, yet they are successful. Same goes for skills. You will find people less skillful than you, but they have reached the peak. It is not always advisable to keep on adding skills where you can find people who can do this for you. What you need is to focus on the active zone i.e. at the levels of your beliefs, values, identity and the big purpose of the life. So, we'll be working on the levels of active zone only, levels of the reactive zone will automatically fall in place.

Now take a step back to enter this active zone of extraordinary people. You have now reached the level of beliefs and values. Find out your beliefs about life. Check out which are the limiting beliefs. Here you may find that you know a little about yourself. This is the shocking truth you may find at this level. You may know a lot of things about other people, political parties, actors, players, etc. but when it comes to yourself you are the most embarrassed person. Try to find out your beliefs about health, relationship, money, career, success, etc. Is there any belief which is stopping you? Just watch from a distance. Don't worry even if you don't get any answers. Next, look for your values and find out what is important to you. Is it health or money or relationship or career or something else? Whatever it is, find out now.

One more step back and you are now at the level of identity. Question yourself who am I? Am I diabetic? Am

I depressed? Am I stupid? Of course not. I may have a challenge of diabetes or depression for some time, but I am not it. I have had none of these earlier and may be after some time, I might not have these again. If I have a car, am I a car you'll drive. If I have a tomato, am I a tomato? Will you make my sauce now? Let's not make our possessions our identity. But the question remains who am I? Ask yourselves, "If my name appears in the dictionary what should have been written in front of it." That is your identity. Let's not dig deep further now and move to the next level.

This is the level where we find our purpose of life i.e. what for we have been sent on this earth. If you imagine that you are sitting somewhere in the sky and from there you can see yourself, find out the reason what for you are here. What is the purpose of your life? Learned people who have been there on this earth till date have mentioned only two big purpose of our life. One we are here for growth - grow in terms of the things which we value. This can be our health, overall happiness, finances, career, relationships, etc. These may be different for different people. Second is the contribution- contribution to this universe. So, we should contribute back to the universe which we are getting from it. This contribution helps us to grow further because the universe always gives us back many folds.

While you are still at the topmost level where you have found the big purpose of the life, imagine that you are living this purpose. Imagine yourself growing in terms of health. See yourself enjoying a sound health; see your doctor is giving you a clean chit after seeing your test reports and saying, you enjoy such a wonderful health. Imagine yourself going to hospitals and other places where you are giving health talks and guiding people how to remain healthy. Imagine yourself enjoying a successful career which you have dreamt. All the people significant to you are appreciating you for the success. Imagine people are asking you for a help in their career and you are happily helping them. Imagine you have all the money you wanted, and you are enjoying a big car, bungalow and whatever you wished for. You are also helping others by donating money to orphanages, old age homes, school and other needy persons. You are bringing the smile on the face of so many people. You are not only helping the persons, but you are helping animals, trees, lakes also. Imagine you are adopting some forests or lakes and doing things for their betterment. You are contributing in whatever way you can. You are enjoying great relationships with your family, friends, and colleagues. As you see yourself growing in these fields which you have wanted, and contributing to this universe, now take a step forward to reach the level of your identity.

Now it is time to make your identity. Imagine that you have a visiting card in your hand on which your name, address, email, phone number etc. are written. You are showing the path to many people, so you are a path changer. You are helping many people in various ways which are bringing smiles to their faces that means you are a smile-generator. You are contributing back to the universe that makes you a contributor. You are changing the lives of millions of people; hence you are a change maker and transformer. Now as you have created this powerful identity of a contributor, path shower, smile generator, change maker and transformer, say it loudly – as loudly as you can – in your mind. Say, I am a change maker. I am a contributor. I am a path shower. I am a smile generator. I am a transformer. Repeat it multiple times in your mind. Now, you are giving a command to the subconscious mind to replace your existing identity with this powerful identity. Spend some time doing this so that it is implanted in your subconscious mind.

Now with this powerful identity, take a step forward to move to the level of beliefs and values. You have earlier made the hierarchy of all of your values. Take your top four or five values out of the list and repeat them loudly in your mind as you have done it for the identity. For example, if your top values are health, relationship, money, success, then say loudly, "For me important is good health and long age; for me important is money; for me important is success; for me important is relationships". Speak as loudly as you can in your mind. Once you are done, then come to your beliefs. Whatever beliefs you might have does not matter as I am giving you the most powerful belief which has helped me at every step of the life and is still helping me. That powerful belief is, "I am the unique child of this universe and this universe is keeping safe in its palms and helping me at every step." Move ahead in life with this powerful belief. This belief will take you to the destination where you have been wishing to reach for so long.

Now move two steps ahead and directly go to the level of your behaviours. With your purpose of life, identity, values, and beliefs which you have just created for yourself, imagine your ideal day. Visualize how and what time you are waking up in the morning? What are the activities you are doing in your ideal day? Imagine yourself doing all the activities important to you (take the top four to five values you have finalized for yourself). See what you are doing to get your results for the things important to you. If you have taken four values, imagine that each week you are taking one value and taking actions to achieve results related to that value.

As I mentioned earlier, I have made you work only on the levels of the active zone as this is the zone where you need to work. You have all the desired levels you need in life as far as the reactive zone is concerned. Moreover, once you have found the big purpose, created your identity, corrected the value hierarchy and gave yourself a powerful belief all the other things will automatically fall into place. Now that you are aligned, you are unstoppable, and life will be smooth and wonderful.

The only thing left now is to go into future and see yourself enjoying your dream life. So, imagine your dream life now i.e. what do you want from this life? You will live the dream life in your mind. Imagine as if you have already achieved your dream life and visualize yourself living the dream life. Now imagine the milestones which will ensure you are in the right direction.

Imagine a straight unending road in front of you. You'll walk on this road now. You may turn on a motivational music in the background. Get ready to live the life you want.

As you start moving on this imaginary timeline, with your eyes closed, see the wonderful unending road ahead of you. Make the road as beautiful as you can. This is your journey. Make it as wonderful as you can imagine. Imagine that a white or golden light in the form of blessings is falling on this unending road thus providing you the energy of this universe to help you in achieving your dreams. Imagine you are meeting all the significant people and your idols on this timeline. Imagine yourself healthy, happy, energetic, young and slim. You are feeling blessed while you are moving ahead.

Now you have reached your first milestone. Let us say this is five years (you may assume as per your plan) ahead from the present. You stop at the milestone to see your name on the milestone. See the script written on the milestone which says you are welcome and congratulations you have achieved your goal set for this milestone. You are thanking the milestone and writing an autograph on it.

Imagine yourself achieving your goal which you have set at this junction. Imagine you are celebrating the success with your family, idols etc. Imagine you are driving a big car and living in a big bungalow. All the significant people are appreciating you. See yourself helping people with money and your knowledge. Whatever you see, make those pictures, bigger, brighter and bolder. Make the sounds louder and intensify all the feelings.

Now you are moving ahead towards the next milestone ten years ahead of the previous one. Here also, milestone is welcoming you and congratulating you. You are thanking this milestone and writing an autograph. Imagine yourself achieving the results you had targeted for this milestone. Imagine yourself throwing a big party where your family, idols and significant people are present. Imagine your idols becoming your fan because of your achievements. In fact, this is the biggest achievement when your idols are becoming your fans. Imagine yourself enjoying good health, a successful career and imagine that you have become financially free. Instead, you are helping others now. Here also, whatever you see, make the pictures, bigger, brighter and bolder. Make the sounds louder and intensify all the feelings.

Now you are moving to the next milestone and you are in your 100^{th}year. Here again, the milestone is welcoming you and congratulating you. You are thanking it also and writing autograph. you are on a vacation with your family and enjoying life to the full extent. Imagine yourself thinking you have been living such a beautiful life. You are thanking your God for this special life. At the hundredth year also, you are still happy, healthy, energetic, young and slim. People are asking the secret of such a wonderful life and you are happily telling them how to live life as you know it.

Now, you are coming back to the present while walking on this blessed and wonderful path. While coming back you are looking at all the milestones and waving them as if you are saying I am coming to you again. Once you reach the present, just keep your both hand at your heart. Let the feelings which you are having at present, flow throughout your body. Intensify these feelings. Keep enjoying these feelings and thank your parents and God to give you such a wonderful life. Keep enjoying for some more time. Now, move your fingers, rub your palms and put them on your face. Slowly open your eyes.

You have everything now using which you can create a life which you have always dreamt. Congratulations, you are all set to live your wonderful life. Follow the techniques mentioned in this book religiously and you will be unstoppable.

PART 3

Time to Act

CHAPTER 11

The Seven Week Challenge

Now, that you know all the seven secrets which can lead to your dream life, it is time to act. Without action, a plan is just a piece of paper. You have understood why some people remain ordinary and some (maybe a few) become extraordinary. These extraordinary people either learn these secrets as you have done, or they unknowingly use these secrets (or you may say they know them at their subconscious level). Your mind is everything. The way you use it, you will become accordingly. Now you know how you can rewire your mind to get rid of unwanted patterns and replace them with the desired patterns of possibilities and opportunities. Once you use these secrets, you will find the appreciable positive change in your life which you will also see in the eyes of other people.

I sum up these secrets for your better understanding. The First secret is you should know where you need to go, else it will be an aimless journey. So, first know your goals. Know what your dream life is? Only knowing is not sufficient, you must have a strong reason- why do you need such a life? Once this is clear, the next step is to make a plan and clear all the objections-internal as well as the external.

Next step is to strengthen the foundation. The secret is to clear all the past burden. If you move forward without doing it, it will always pull you back again. So, what you need to do is to remove all the garbage in terms of painful memories, fears, etc. You know the technique now. Make yourself emotional resilient so that you do not get hurt by the verbal attacks of other people. These two secrets make your foundation unshakable.

After strengthening the foundation, you need to create a zone of excellence. First, create inner excellence by building a powerful self-image and learning to be in the groove so that you are always in a state of positivity. Apart from this, create a rapport with the people. Identify their representational system and communicate by entering their internal world. Use the mirroring technique as well to strengthen the rapport.

Align all of your neurological levels and work in the active zone to create an impact. Break all the limiting beliefs, clear your value hierarchy, make a power identity and live the big purpose of life. Live your dream life daily in your mind. Make a two minute mental movie and run this movie every morning and also in the night before you sleep.

I have given you the tools which will help you in realizing your dreams and to make you live a life which you have been striving for so long. Now it is up to you how well do you use these. If you read it just as another book, I am sure it will not help. Consider this book as a workshop which will convert you into a totally different person – a better version of your present 'you'. I suggest you take this as a challenge now and convert it into a seven-week plan. Take one secret every week, implement it on yourself and master that secret. After some time, these techniques will become a way of life for you and you will use them without even knowing consciously.

Before implementing I request you to clear all the concepts and techniques so that there is no margin of error. You can record the commands of techniques in your own voice and then play so that you are relaxed while doing it. I wish, the techniques, which I have told you in this book, have a significant positive impact on your life and you get successful in achieving your dream life. I pray to Almighty to always keep you happy and healthy, and May you live a life which you have dreamt.

About the Author

Nilesh Goswami is a certified Stress Management Professional from ICSMP (International Council of Stress Management Professionals), Sydney, a certified NLP Coach, and Memory Trainer. He is an ex Indian Engineering Services officer and MBA (Gold Medallist). He is also a member of the International Stress Management Association (ISMA), India.

Nilesh has a rich experience of over 19 years and has worked with many organizations of repute such as Indian Ordnance Factories (Ministry of Defence Production), Power Grid Corporation of India Ltd., National Institute of Technology, Kurukshetra, Reliance Infrastructure Limited and Bharti Infratel Ltd. During these years, he has been helping people to come out of their life-related issues. This experience has given him a leading edge to understand and resolve issues of his clients. He has been empowering people and organizations through his unique scientific methods of coaching and counselling.

Nilesh is the Founder and Managing Director of the 'Turning Point' which provide Individuals and organizations with the opportunity to thrive through promoting their well-being, and managing stress and psychosocial risks. The company is committed to the overall well-being of individuals and the organizations and to help them live a wonderful life. His mission is to make the life of people beautiful by helping them to achieve the peak performance in all the fields be it in health, relationships, finances or career. His motto is to bring smiles back into our client's life- not only by removing their past pains but also by making the present better along with creating positive patterns for the future.